PROVISIONS OF LIGHT

Provisions
of Light

Tessa Rose Chester

Oxford   New York
OXFORD UNIVERSITY PRESS
1996

Oxford University Press, Walton Street, Oxford OX2 6DP

Oxford New York
Athens Auckland Bangkok Bogota Bombay
Buenos Aires Calcutta Cape Town Dar es Salaam Delhi
Delhi Florence Hong Kong Istanbul Karachi
Kuala Lumpur Madras Madrid Melbourne
Mexico City Nairobi Paris Singapore
Taipei Tokyo Toronto
and associated companies in
Berlin Ibadan

Oxford is a trade mark of Oxford University Press

First published in Oxford Poets
as an Oxford University Press paperback 1996

British Library Cataloguing in Publication Data
Data available

Library of Congress Cataloging in Publication Data
Chester, Tessa.
Provisions of light / Tessa Rose Chester.
p.   cm.
I. Title.
PR6053.H457P76   1996   821'.914—dc20   96–11594
ISBN 0-19-283262-X

10 9 8 7 6 5 4 3 2 1

Typeset by Rowland Phototypesetting Limited
Printed in Hong Kong

For Ron, who seeks light
and for Nan and Vera, who provide it

ACKNOWLEDGEMENTS

Acknowledgements are made to the editors of the following magazines and publications in which some of these poems first appeared: *Bound Spiral, The Bridport Prize, 1994, Envoi, The Genie and the Bottle: Poems from the Open Poetry Competition 1994, Norwich Writers' Circle, Poetry Review, The Rialto, The South West Poetry Anthology '93*. 'Rooms' won joint first prize in the Blue Nose Poets of the Year Competition, 1994.

CONTENTS

The Artist's Wife

'An active line on a walk'—Paul Klee

My line returns from its walk
more smudged than I remember,

blurred by continuing rain.
Almost a wash of grey.

Dressed in several charcoal veils
it appears insubstantial,

needing more emphasis
around the eyes, the breast.

Its ashy curves
slip deep like a river

down stairs to the gloomy place
where I have been waiting

to draw this wet vein,
this dark blood

into my arms again.

Box

For John Lawrence, wood-engraver

A calm, still room. Prepared. Rows
of polished gravers, spitsticks,
scorping tools ready to make
rounds and lozenges and squares.
The plump sandbag bears the block:
seasoned for seven years the
old way, in a cool earth pit,

the grain burns with energy,
red-gold, sweet and dark. It seems
inappropriate to start.
Rough outlines; some initial
scraping, this for water, this
for sky. Now the images
are teased out by the pressure

of the hand; the eye close, fixed,
calculating the precise
danger of the tapering
line, the keen, exquisite thrill
of the deliberate burr.
Relishing the sudden snap
of wood flying past the cheek.

Revealed first are choppy waves,
a seascape of Biblical
aspect, with an ark, a storm
in progress under heavy
cloud, jagged rocks, and two drowned
sailors dancing with mermaids
on the ocean bed. Rainbows

then appear, borders full of
tumbling pigs and cows that pass
the goat with a funny eye
who butts a tabby cat down
through the farmyard scattering
speckled hens. Notice how the
cobbles glisten after rain.

The main theme; village gossip
mixed with urban dialogue.
Deserted parks, terraced streets
in snow, oil on the canal,
cracked but gleaming tiles, sooty
chimney-pots: detail, something
of a speciality.

He likes the intimate scene,
and sets his own dog before
a sparking fire, a friend's grand-
son hurrying home from school.
And down here on the right are
his parents, on a picnic
at a local beauty spot,

watching their boy as he rolls
over and over down the
steep slope, almost off the edge.
Here and there are sprinkled stars
and bubbling trout, catkins with
silky fur, chunks of oak and
elm, a bush of holly, beech

leaves crisp with frost. He slowly
pricks and lures out a lively
conversation, the bustle
of the world in miniature,
domestic and magical
events linked by the constant
speech of countryside and town.

The pull is perfect: deep black,
on paper sharp as ice. Each
drop and whisker visible,
even to delight on the
face of the boy on the hill,
the hill named after the wood
from which this rare block was cut.

Lights

1

A large, square country house at night.
Plain, whitewashed walls
with closed green shutters

and a grey roof that will
green with the dawn.
The old lamp before the house

drips pale yolk
into a pond (or stream,
it's difficult to tell),

the wall creaming gold
from the lamp's buttery heart.

Birch or alder at the water's edge
stretch up through blue sky,
showering the house with dark lace.

The light breeze
tomorrow will toss
the trees into autumn,

shooing the clouds on
to another day,
another fluffy noon.

Sometimes this painting drifts out.
It enters eyes
where it trembles,

humming in an egg-shell sleep.

Sometimes it sits
quite quietly,
floating on its thoughts.

*

No door is shown.
Only the blank, lit wall
and the shutters; but

upstairs, two windows glow
like ripened fruit.

Someone is about to get up
and walk across that room
where a fire burns.

There may be a scream,
a flash, a thud:
the sudden gulp of light

downed in one.
Or perhaps, someone will lean
back in their chair and sigh.

Then nothing more.

2
This room has a bed,
a chair, a writing-desk.
Wood-smoke comfortably

scents the midnight air.
At dawn, leaf-green stripes
cross the polished floor,

hovering round the bed,
minting the cool sheets.
Hands, feet bathe in light.

During the day
quick steps come and go,
waiting on the invalid

in buttercup and cream;
rustling aprons
like old leaves,

the heavy swish of
crimson skirts settling
when others have gone.

Hidden birds deliver
scraps of psalms
through half-open blinds

filtering daylight
past its final hours.

And when lamps are lit,
rounded figures
swim in tangerine,

movements
soft as shadows,
melting into prayer.

3
Village lights
burn hazily,

straightening ragged lanes,
tracing the shop, the square;
celebrating monuments.

Holding down
a mass of country black
with white-water weight.

Travellers
passing quickly
through this wide night

see tinsel string the valley,
tiny stars punctuating
the deep negative
of riding to an unknown end.

*

What do these lights mean to you?

The glow behind the curtain
of a house that is not yours.

The dwindling light of the ghost
who is not appreciated.

Invisible light
eluding brush and lens
or tips of the finest wing.

Lights of a season, an age,
the colours of our moods,
our heated, frozen breath.

Lights that leak
the shapes our shadows are.

4
Although Magritte painted
L'empire des lumières
several times,

the beauty
remains resolute,
contained.

Looking at this painting
more than twenty years ago,
a great distance separated us.

It sat
in the corner of the hall
like a quiet bomb.

Unknown to others
I was carrying you;
at eighteen, knowing little

but the dark cough
from my father's lung,
the keening of a cold year.

Now, looking for the second time,
I feel again that same
dumb fullness,

sense of things
waiting to arrive.

This house,
this lamp,
this pool of light

watering the path.
Reflections quivering
behind our eyes

as we turn to face
the black, sluggish Thames
and count the lights

littering the London sky.

Ben

on your second birthday

O doughty traveller!
Keeper of the rainbow boots.
Master of tactics
manoeuvring ranks of relatives
in flushed pursuit.
Tough as it takes,
cannon-fire at dawn,
clarion call for larks.
Busy with paints and drill,
ironing fit to kill.

Yet soft as cheese,
born sunny-side up
and buoyant as a red balloon.
Bubbling box of tricks;
word-juggler,
chef of the participle.
Punchy as a bean-bag,
warm as winter toast.
Small explosion,
home-grown
bomb.

A Candle at Canterbury

For Muriel

1 *Rye harbour, night*

Marshland merges with a tarry sea.
A long, thin road bleeds into the sky,
the only life-line on a palm empty

of all promise. I stand, terrified.
The infinite depth, the infinite height
of blackness, with its sole unblinking eye

The Fisherman's Rest, burning through a night
I never wanted to confront alone.
Yet here I am. I keep the car in sight

and call my mother from the public phone
whose solid presence strangely dignifies
my fear, makes it respectable. Her tone

of voice confirms a death. So: yet more ties
with childhood cut. Perhaps the distant scenes
I can recall will serve to exorcise

my blurred, unfamiliar aunt. I have jeans
and grass-stained trainers, odd socks, anorak.
I don't have either will or extra means

to purchase petrol, or funereal black.
She says there is no need to come: somehow
I feel quite uninvolved; the slap and tack

of water thickening on an unseen bow
is all I hear, that matters, anyhow.

11

2 Canterbury

Passing down the great cathedral's throat
I shift the dark. A cough of shadows
is released and in slow motion floats

about a gasp of nuns and widows
sunk upon their polished agate knees,
impressive in this genuflecting pose;

even dust clouds sparkle with their pleas,
illuminating prayers in blue and gold.
I stand aloof. What's this to do with me,

an atheist for years; my god grew old
and withered when my father died. But here,
watching all these pilgrims newly souled,

I turn towards the sputtering bank and clear
a space; take a candle; speak a name;
set light within a hundred lights, a bier

of incandescent holy-water flame.
We sit, the dead and I. There is no blame.

3 *Rye harbour, dawn*

It's the last, the very last place on earth
to want to be. I find the pub asleep,
the same huge stillness waiting for the birth

of sound. Even the solitary gull keeps
counsel as he wheels once then dips again,
a little boat beached well within his sweep.

Funerals are not my scene; since the rain
drowned my father's January flowers
and drained his cards of our final words; pain

made worse by undiscriminating showers.
Families are so much rotten news;
at least, I can't explain the strain in ours.

My given name is all I have to lose.
I find it, suddenly, on hull and sail
of this small boat. It's a sign, but on whose

side? At this low ebb of mine, on this pale
beach, is there, have I still time to fail?

The Gallery

Old Hall, South Burlingham.
For Margaret Steward and Peter Scupham

I wear my easy face for you.
You're privileged to stand unharmed

within this half-light yawn,
the runt of a September day.

My last sightings? Butterflies
hot with rusty blood, black clots

frilled blue, their tender belly-fuzz
still warm; engraved in plaster flakes

they decorate my under-skirts,
trimmed with grit; antennae cocked

to catch each insubstantial breath,
to charge each footstep dragging by.

See how cobwebbed tributaries
map my bulging walls; come, squeeze

your fist into these gaping wounds
through which the thatch thrusts its reedy

fingers, greedily. Wait till
the ashes of the night catch fire,

then I'll gather all my hounds
about me, set the hunt alight!

Where are your shields, your quivering spears,
my fine Elizabethan men?

Where are the roses for your dogs,
the horn to sound the rallying-cry?

(You see these rigid eyes? This man
prepares to kill). On moonlit nights

we sail this great grey galleon down
the attic rivers, curtained ports,

velvet shadows in our wake
as we circumnavigate

the tendrilled, daisy-painted stairs
fanning deep into the dark green

throat of the sleeping house. It stirs,
dreaming of a mermaid song while

tossing on an ocean of fine
print, curlicues and fishes' tails.

The seafolks' enigmatic gaze
calms the whiskers of the guardian

cats, the Four who watch and wait, their
golden spirits murmuring spells

to ring this place. I pass them by,
a smile upon my easy face.

The Intimacies of Lilith

Magnolia skin
moistened by midnight rain.

Dark breasts, swinging
slightly as she sings.

That hint of blood to come
in deep hollows;
the tips of hairs stinging
down her arms, wrists, ankles, feet.

Warm swathes of hair
fingering her bent neck
in a blind massage.

Knowing just where to go,
how fast to pace it;
when to slow.

An easy velvet elasticity,
the flowering of the crimson labial tongue
from which her ancient perfumes run.

Milk, honey-thick and glorious,
creaming in-between her thighs.

She retracts, expands:
the air fills with incense
and sagacious mists,

each sense translated
into one cyclonic pulsar
of immense girth and strength.

She tastes salt, honey, blood, ice;
sweet lustrous waters.

Her body is a sponge for earthly fluids.
Her mind can conduct aerial messages,

communicating with the smallest
moth or mountain, oak or stone.

Rivers pour out of her.

She has extraordinary skills,
extreme abilities.

She can accomplish miracles;
change water into fire,
white to black.

She has become as black as night

while the thousand children in her
are giving birth to stars.

What Happened Outside Nick's Bar at 2 am After the Late Movie in a Sleazy Little Town Somewhere Off the Highway

We pause in the wake of the neon sign.
She shifts close, warm,
teasing me with a sideways glance.
When we kiss
her fingers curve round my crotch
almost as an after-thought.
Her breasts flash tangerine
plum   tangerine   plum
and taste as bitter as sloes.

I fuck her up against the wall,
adjusting to the pulse
of the flickering light.
Against her saffron throat her hair lies
like a crimson scarf
but her eyes and mouth are black.

I lean over her,
taking the strain on my left arm
while my right hand kneads
her mottled breasts.
As I quicken, thrusting deep,
her face becomes a movie screen
shot with tangled images
in sweating, inky pools;
down beneath her eyes
I drum her bones,
drown her drumming bones
while the audience beat time
and their eyes and mouths are black.

As I straighten up
she drops
like a bruised fruit
at my feet.

And I run like hell.

Provisions of Light
Sole Bay, Suffolk

First day
Thin masks of white light,
layers of pallid space

that could be sky or land
or something in-between;

a yawn,
a week-old cry.

A huge brightness,
hanging

on a coast
dipped in ice,

as frail and mutable
as sculpted sand.

*

Ties of river, sea and creek
make Southwold almost an island,

one road out, one road in
passing straight down through

cafés and boutiques to the beach,
the famous lighthouse an

overpowering tower of snow
on a March day that thinks it's June.

On Sunday, Jack taps his bell
for church and inn alike,

19

keeping Shakespeare's stroke
between plea and meditation

while vat-full cottages
steam in the sun,

Adnam's beer running
warm in local veins.

*

Do not walk the seven Greens,
on East or North,

Bartholomew or Barnaby,
Tibby's or St James's,

not even on the cool curved
cushions of South Green:

do not walk, for you will burn
your feet on others' bones,

they are swollen with ashes
from the Great Fire of 1659.

There are cold ghosts, too,
for foggy nights

when shrieking women run about Gun Hill
and drowned sailors

shuffle dripping to the Lion
or stride, headless,

down forgotten alleyways
to leave forecasts of death.

But now, in early Spring,
on a day streaming with light,

rusty dogs make the most
of freedom on the beach,

crunching pebbles,
snorting North Sea foam that lies

about the patchy sand like shaving cream.
The wide shingle shelves

glint with pale buff and coral stones,
sugared almonds, temporary gems.

Second day
Walking alone on the shore
under a bruised sky,

the marsh filled with mist.
Headphones ring with Philip Glass

on piano, *Opening;*
rippling waves of notes

suggest the sleekness of seals,
satin tuxedos, an echoing hall.

There is an absence of colour,
the total absence of smell,

the sea slushing to the left,
reeds concealed to the right,

sky and sea reduced
to overlapping greys:

impressions of a *film noir*
with unseen actors, whispering.

I cannot truly say
I have been a woman; a mother;

a daughter; a wife;
not even a poet.

I could say, I have lived,
but in what sense.

Only that I breathed,
and that I tried as hard as anyone

and lost as much.
And you would say the same.

Are the records we make enough
to give substance to our memory?

Are words and pictures ever enough
to build more than silhouettes?

Have we left some deed
of natural grace behind,

moments when the trying became
active accomplishment

instead of the faint trace
of love we might have given

if we had only stopped recording
for an instant.

So much time wasted
while the present

passes with each step
and the shutter jams a future

in which there is
no more film.

*

Along the harbour,
intersecting horizontals, verticals,

hard streaks of black
slice water, sky and land

into geometric shapes
of varying size.

There is a calming pattern
to these rules:

the clean line of sail and mast,
rope and post, hull and wing,

the rows of closed-up huts,
discarded boards, uneven planks;

kinetic strings
playing against the wind.

Not much is happening here
though *Christina Clara* opens early

for fresh crab. The boats convalesce,
nursing last year's wounds:

Boy John, *Thistle*,
Prospero and *Billyboy*,

rocking slightly
in their muddy beds.

Third day

The Amber shop glows
with electrifying power.

Sacred jewel of Apollo
and the tribe of Benjamin,

cast here as trinkets for the rich.
Drops of clear honey,

red-gold ovals, whisky-coloured
beads in their thousands

decorate the room,
an orchestra of liquid light.

Here is jewellery to dress the ear,
the neck, the arm,

each finger or wrist.
Here are ornaments to dress rooms

with leaves or fruit
on silver trees, exotic animals

for that occasional stand
or table in the vestibule.

The assistant is in black
and thinks you cannot pay.

With his accounting mind
he sets a tiny rabbit in your palm,

then rough rocks of original stone.
You go for one trawled locally,

a swadge of lemon cheese
with ribbed and barnacled rind

and a neat depression
where your thumb can rest.

Though smooth as glass
it's warm to touch,

absorbing the scent of your skin.
You want it to smell of the sea.

Fourth day
Town-dwellers soon forget the darkness
of the countryside; how to see stars,

how to steer one's way
through deep black gulfs.

Blythburgh church is lighthouse to the marsh,
a luminary on solid ground

that can be seen for miles
at night, and in the day stands

reflected in the pools of Angels Marsh
and in the river Blyth.

Inside, the light intensifies
against the lime-washed walls,

the high roof spanned by angels
with pitted faces.

Carved poppy-heads represent
sins and seasons in more human form,

while the Great North Door
bears the Devil's mark from 1577

when he 'rent the timber, brake the chimes'
and left a boy 'starke dead'.

*

Down the road at Wenhaston
devils stir again

in the Doom painting
of a medieval monk.

His furry demon even now disturbs,
staring out of the fish's mouth

with eyes like lorry lamps,
his yellow mouth agape.

It's easy to imagine him
scuttling about his business at night.

Fifth day
At Dunwich there is more
space than form.

The light is dull,
evaporating sluggishly

from centuries of conflict
with the sea.

This eating of the land,
each relentless push,

the constant rub and scour
that turns grand buildings

into gravel, sucks the colour
from the fishing fleets,

the barges, warehouses
and mills of a once great port,

that drags the palace,
chapel, church,

monastery and school,
hospice and inn,

brass city gate,
stone wall and street,

deep down into a square mile
of water we have so polluted

since that divers have to
extract objects by touch,

where the ghosts of monks
mingle with sailors,

merchants, soldiers,
maybe even a king.

The sea creates its own
dark, encrusted furniture

out of the ruins of the land,
once applauded masonry

engraved with fishes' bite,
the slow slow nibble of the tide.

A sonorous clang is sometimes heard,
hidden bells calling the litany

of the lost:
chapels of St Francis,

Katherine, Anthony,
churches of St Bartholomew,

Leonard, Martin,
Michael and Felix,

Patrick and Mary,
Nicholas and John,

St Peter, and the rare
round church

of the Knights Templars.
All Saints was the last,

sliding away
a mere ninety years ago,

leaving just one
grave behind

in half a wood
on half a cliff.

No need now for Dunwich men
to harass Southwold

for harbour mastery;
the ports have gone,

the only trade
being in tourist bone,

the bleached bones
of bishops and kings,

fragments of arm or thigh
revealed by yet another storm,

ivory skulls
on the beach

or studding the cliff,
faces within a face.

*

Travelling here
you carried

shreds of pain,
self-degrading doubts,

and found a coast
soaked with spirits

of both light and dark,
a place of slow loss and

fading brilliance,
where the heron's

easy circling flight
stays etched

in a purity of air,
where the villages

and towns swim in glass,
leaking colour

to the sea.
You return with images

of waste, exile
and despair,

the little Wenhaston devil
snuffling at your heels.

But in your palm
you hold excavated light,

the amber wedge healing
while there is still time,

infused with
the luminosity

of Suffolk sky and sea,
keeping your writing fingers warm.

Running Hares
A Winter Convalescence

These clothes don't fit.
You packed odd socks, tatty pants;
pale stains from a previous flesh.

Trust you to get it wrong.
I want things new
to comfort vulnerable skin.

Not that I look that different,
you understand,
but deep inside

past all the little gates
of knitted silk,
I'm freshly pruned and strung,

cut like the wind
that shapes the fen
where I walk each day

with only the low red sun
to see, and hares
running in the snow.

Buttons

Appointment on a rainy afternoon:
a way to heal relationships, he said.
She felt like drowning in the fluid gloom;

this was worse than anything she'd read.
He told them to relax; brought out a box;
explained the button game. Removed the lid.

At once I'm kneeling by a fire, my socks
alive with twitchy sparks. Gritty grains
of coal scratch my legs, hidden in the flock

of great-grandmother's rug. The window-panes
creak with frost. My mother sews above
me, talking on and off. She has to crane

her neck to see how I am. It's enough
just to be part of this transient thumbnail
scene. I warm my toes. She darns her glove.

Through my fingers buttons click like hail:
a steel sonata for the avant-garde,
a trickling glockenspiel, an echoing bell.

Glazy eyes cast rainbows, delicately starred.
I stroke their bones with my thumb: fabric flutes
and gills, some marble-smooth, some ribbed and barred.

Buttons fill small hands. Jade-green balls, coot-
black beads, globules of watery glass,
purple berries, tarnished moons in pewter-

grey, tiny plastic red and yellow hearts.
I lay them out as offerings around
my mother's feet. Fragile cameos, brass

pennies, copper clover-leaves, pearl fish wound
about with faded thread. Row on row
encircling us. Strange how trivial things resound

with vibes, percussive magic deep and slow.
Sorting buttons into lives, making sense
of self through patterning. Now I know.

She makes her choice. He cannot recompense
her for lost years, there's nothing to retrieve.
Rising, buttons spill, but she's caught the scent

of freshened futures. So much to achieve
without old ties! There'll be no time to grieve.

At 'Relate', couples may be asked to choose the buttons they think
most resemble each other.

Aspects of Amnesia

1 A Minute Memory

In your head, once:

wooden ships
and painted umbrellas.
Glass globes full of rain.
Illuminated maps with
speech paths pricked in red,
rivers of syllables in blue.

In your head, once:

placards from a friendly town.
Rooms of waterfalls
and drizzling snakes.
A dictionary forest
black with argument.
Doors to a million swimming-pools.

In your head, once:

throats of nightingales;
the ghost of a golden tamarin.
A face, a number, a voice
tied up in musically-scented ribbon.
Scraps of a ballad
in lavender and cream.

In your head, now:

a present cleaned of context.
Sixty-second chunks
of anaesthetized events.
A mute rush hour
you can never join.
False familiarity.

The cold, still horror
of sleep without a dream,
of a disinfected name
that might, or might not,
be yours.

2 *The Continuous Search for Proof*

Of the reputation of birds;
the fragility of flowers, and skin.

Of the basic principles of flight;
of the texture of stones, and snow.

Of the strict arrangement of rooms,
the possession of table and chair.

Of the consolation of touch
and the natural conditions for sleep.

Of the need to wash both your hands
and the tedious constrictions of dress.

Of the sequence of sock and shoe.
Of the sequence of sock and shoe.

That the face in the mirror is known.
That the face in the mirror is you.

3 *Ritual*

'Rosy apple, mellow pear,
Bunch of roses she shall wear;
Gold and silver by her side;
I know who shall be my bride.'

At a beech desk
by the window

you hum your writing tune.
The words 'rose' and 'apple'

sink into paper
thick as cream.

You draw their letters
round and large

with infinite care.
The faint dragging

of the pen;
a small clock, somewhere.

The evening sun
ageing each page

of the amber manuscript,
spilt light

trickling through
'o's' and 'p's'

like lost diacritics,
capillaries of stress.

The words grow and grow,
apple, rose.

Each filled sheet
flung aside,

forgotten.
Milky leaves

lie about the dark floor
like slivered ice.

And always that hypnotic,
measured hum:

'Rosy apple, mellow pear,
Bunch of roses she shall wear . . .'

*

A woman enters the room.
She is elderly.

She speaks to you
and tells you she is your mother.

The humming stops.
The pen stops.

Your hands perform
like birds, quick with fear.

When the pen falls,
the woman picks it up

and as she hands it to you
there is a smell of musk,

a hint of cloves and thyme.
From the deep, green pockets

of her skirt
she pulls fruit and flowers,

but you turn away.
When she sings your song

you start to draw again,
bold hoops, great rings

wider, taller,
plump bowls holding

seas of soft chalk,
an acreage of snow.

Apple, rose.
Apple, rose.

*

A woman enters the room.
She speaks to you, quietly.

She is old
and says she is your mother,

and you recall
a warm, brown, loamy smell.

She comes back later.
You still sit

by the window
at a shadowy desk

with your papers
crumbled ash

in the corners of the room,
but each time she is just

an old woman with wet eyes
who says she is your mother,

and whose skin smells
of small gardens,

musk, and thyme, and cloves.
'Mother' is just a word.

Like apple.
Like rose.

4 *Litany of Loss*
Not the balance of eye and hand,
or how to make strings vibrate.
Not the notes of Ravel's Pavane,
the fingering of a duet.

Not the passion for abstract art,
or for rhymes or games or balloons;
the madrigal's intricate parts,
or how to play bells, or tap spoons.

But the distinction of character.
The capacity for love.
The confidence of friends.

The reasoning for thought.
The infidelity of truth.
The experience to doubt.

The requirements of custom.
The particulars of faith.
The perception of cant.

The progression of time.
The ordering of days.
The desire for death.

Insomnia

The intensity of the silence
pushes you deeper
into your little house of voices:
a dolls' house made of TV sets
tuned to different channels
alternating loud and soft;
vibrations rattling their tin hearts.

Unfinished songs clamour for your ears.
Can you hear the nursery rhyme your mother sang,
oh lullaby of rings and waves?
Or the sound of the organ playing at your wedding
through the white fizz of candles and choirs?
Or the aria of spindrift flowers
your first love drank from the sand?
And in the distance, sad fluttering birds
continue to call.

Do you hear them?

Half-heard phrases slipping by
cannot be caught.
All the unsaid words in the world
are jangling jigsaws in your head,
too faded to see
and never complete.
The colours that flash about you
like tempests of fire
are celebrating a festival of blood.
With sparkling sabres they fight
the beat of your heart.

And the running of your feet
through the corridors
through the dolls' house rooms
through the tunnels with no air
can never escape

the challenge of the sun.

Rooms

1 The Hall of Unknown Projections

A strange room hands no map
to those born blind.
New constructions must be learned
by the tilt of the light,
a temperamental draught;
constants that plot initial shape.

This house is shuffling its thermographs.

Extend your arms:
test each bronze weight,
the depth of grainy wells.

Stepping out
is like entering a pool
of ruffled feathers,
warm and cold in turn,
and currents tug you
over here or there
to note the furniture,
the mass of stair.

Now the mapping is complete
the hall's veins fill
with what you think is red or blue,
while pale gold spills on your face
from that indeterminable space above.

2 The Snow Salon

Archways to the right lead
gently to a suite of snows
with alabaster columns,
empty ivory alcoves.

It has been growing light in here for centuries.

Dust, fine as face-powder,
settles snowy layers on
the sleek chill of frosted sheets,
a satin, lilied ottoman,
smooth hills of writing-desk and chair.

Crushed echoes hang
like chandeliers.

Hushed clocks.

An unplayed piano
one more hummock
on a ground of Paris white.

Whatever lives have been
are made invisible
by amnesiac cold,

and you feel a sudden weariness
watching filmy walls dissolve and re-appear
in anaesthetic mime.

You must sleep now,
here in this snowing globe,
and search among impressions
for angelic shapes,
the one still warm,
hoping that your arms
will fit its absent wings.

3 *The Dome of Beauties*

The vast curving sky
drops coloured light down
as little birds,
and you walk through slim rainbows
with glowing hands,
yellow tipped with rose,
fluttering.

The rotunda has a richness
formed by natural light,
the sun on stained glass
illuminating hangings round the wall:
gold and crimson tapestries
with sinuous, silky dragons
burning through a night of silver moons.

Here and there
a porcelain dish,
stupendous vases
on which peonies and chrysanthemums
curl in lush exuberance;
nests of ebony tables;
boxes, intricately carved
with cherry trees and waves,
sparrows in the rain,
shapely clouds, holy men,
amber lanterns marking out
the thousand flowered way upon a lake.

All this beauty pours into
a room that is familiar,
and you turn slowly
through the dizzy spectrum
like a chameleon,
tracing lovely things
without knowing
they are yours.

4 Ballroom

Glass-gold explosions.
Deep red curtain-falls.
Glittering mirrors,
crystal and brocade.

A room fit for kings
with unseen dancers
from another time.

Powders, perfumes, oils and sweat
alert you to a polka hurricane:
a clutch of heavy silks, a rush of lace,
fine hairs light upon your arm.
Urgent whisperings
thick with lacquer and exotic spice,
sticky syllables of gossip
hovering in the close, magnetic air
while behind you
murmurings prowl
as soft as milk.

You are unnoticed,
blundering about the floor
from one embrace
to another,
wondering which of you
is the ghost.

5 The Corridor of Serious Pursuits

A thousand gilt-edged tomes
in towering stacks;
unrelenting rows
closing in to left and right.

Their cinnamon and umber uniforms
emit a curiously oppressive smell,
your startled cough
constricting regulation spines.

Questions clog the air,
but a search reveals
works of solemn emptiness,
dummies, masquerading
as a collection of great lives.

6 *The Chamber of Indelicate Lies*

This room is full. Hot.
Bordello-red.
The velvet walls have eyes—
quick, when they turn away.

Quick,
I have urgent business
and I want no questions asked.

We have mouths to swap
and flesh to superintend,

anything to pass the time
while it's still warm.

The air shakes with its own pulse.

When the bed creaks,
remember to breathe.

7 *The Attic*

Little vague crumbling things:
ashy moths,
bones of butterflies.

Bits of cloth, stained scraps.
Burnt primrose papers
with their crackling messages:

to my darling . . .
will I see you . . .
forever . . .
yes

why?

The Why whisper,
hanging from a butcher's hook.
Whys
dripping from a beam
onto piles of penny magazines,
one clumpy shoe,
a china doll
in its original box;

the sudden red of horses' hooves,
an army in a canvas bag;
that cloak of such momentous blue;
the lost wheel of the discarded trike.

Each small betrayal of those summery years
reduced to this desiccated heap,

dry nests of memory.

8 The Waiting-Room

So few things are needed
for a waiting-room.
A table, perhaps.

Chairs.
Many chairs
set round a large central area
on which to meditate.

After a while
you begin to observe
the intimate lives of small beasts;

at your feet
the legs of unfortunate flies
continue to twitch.

The spider also waits.

*

After a long while,
waiting
becomes an end in itself.

You are there,
and nothing else exists;
no time, no reason.

Simply a room
with table and chairs.

*

Finally
you become aware
that some disintegration has occurred:
a century of seasons in faded, rotten parts;

the time-lapsed fragmentations of the human will
through which you sit, unmoved.

When the light gives,
you're left standing in the dark,
listening,
trying to sort new maps,
different shades of absence.

Casting about for familiar shapes
on the edge of space,
hearing only your wild heart

beating

through your finger-tips.

December Wedding

For Emma, James, and Ben, 19.12.94

A room of heavy beams,
ropes and planks;
a swelling ship
full of strangers.

Change.

Muslin spreads like foam,
weeds of emerald ribbon
coil around the balustrade.
Pagan greenery bursts
from the tight warmth of shadows.

The cake is an arctic sea:
penguin, whale and bear
on ice-blue floes
etched with a letter, a name,
waves of thin gold thread.

Now the special glitter
worn by Christmas nights
creeps over our uncertain mood,
its sharp, frosted scent
like hyacinths unfolding in the snow.

When the white car comes
these changes hang like little fires
in the December dusk.

When the white car comes
it brings man, woman, child.

The confidential man
is yet unfathomed, grave.
The fir-boned woman
has a dress of rich ocean green,

the deep green of forests after rain.
Her amber neck, arms, breast,
seem malleable, kissable.
She has light shining in her,
out of her,
and the child's clear eyes
reflect street-lamps in
a heady jazz of stars.

As night comes thick and low,
man, woman and child
move around by candle-light,
a trinity of gold and green
in a dazzle of rings.

They keep close counsel,
guarded by their thoughts.

We present our gifts like awkward magi:
wood, silver, glass;
mirrors to aid domestic spells.

Later, the Old Magic will see
wolf and fir running in a place
to which we cannot go:

there they will deal in
the transposition of dark bloods,
in the reordering of family stars

within a circle of water and flame
cupped by two small hands.

Twelfth Night

A measure of snow
  in the difficult dark

A measure of dark
  for the tree's distress

A measure of distress
  at the turning year

cut-glass birds
on their last flight
losing their sheen

the finality of flame
deepening the night
the absence of green

A measure of sorrow
A measure of snow

The Minden Sonnets

1

If it's a question of leaving, just go.
Bludgeoned by silly words, that nagging need.
When blood is roused by every verbal blow

and we allow each other to misread
our actions. When we will not, cannot stop;
when we kill anything that moves. Go, feed

the cat, pack bags, go. Let others prop
the family up. Cut loose, take slow ways down
to catch the season's smell, the smoky drops

of rain, the aromatic breath of towns.
Primeval longing speaks from other years
but I hesitate, almost turning round.

Sehnsucht pulls my understanding clear.
To want something this much; to be this near.

2

To want something this much; to be this near,
trying to summon precious texts by name.
Drawn compulsively from Chichester

to Pevensey through earth-bound links, chains
of church and castle, Iron Age hill-fort,
chorused like a children's singing-game:

Cissbury Ring, Devil's Dyke, Ditchling, Firle. Taut
bronze beacons whirl above the flowery hush
of villages. Flint-and-brick wall the court-

house, cottage, school, while ancient beech and brush
mask the mythical Green Man lying low.
Ask a boy the way to Birling Gap. Crush

shingle in your hand, snuff the air, follow
the confluence of water and the crow.

3

The confluence of water and the crow.
The ghosts of shepherds on the South Downs Way,
counting-out from Went Hill to Haven Brow.

The succulence of limpet-pie, bouquet
of periwinkles from the farm. Shell
and gull in every field. The slow decay

along the coast, fragile darkness of Belle
Tout, Seven Sisters in their blood-stained shifts
crumbling passively under the swell

of moons and tides. Go where dunlin drift
among fleshy sea-plants, glasswort, aster;
the salt-marsh estuary, where redshank sift

for worms in muddy creeks. Pallid Cuckmere,
river of the calligraphic signature.

4

River of the calligraphic signature,
vast shining loop of pastoral elegance
etching marsh and meadow: its allure

inducing a controlled hypnotic trance
round Alfriston. June: the cloudy Tye
billows cotton-wool; summer brilliance

clarifies the white wood bridge, Plonk Barn's flight
of snowy doves, geese in a protective fan.
Through golden wheat to Lullington; close by,

the chalky footpath to the giant Long Man
of Wilmington. Up on Windover Hill
there is unburdening. Test your wingspan

for the coming age! Stretch out all sense, feel
the earth's muscles flexing our free-will.

5

The earth's muscles flexing. Our free-will
discharged by rhythms from historic hours:
tremor of rock, stammer of stone; fibril

energies, minute pulsating showers
barely registered. Invisibles we
refuse to name, yet which contain such power.

To rest; down to Litlington for tea.
Meditate on autumn's weeping bruise
beneath the cawing monkey-puzzle tree.

Clap cups; shake rain; chase yesterday's news
rusting away in amber leaves. Mature
here slowly, meld with umber shadows, lose

your conscious self on purpose to ensure
tranquillity becomes a ligature.

6

Tranquillity becomes a ligature
of dreams I am reluctant to dispel;
far better this than having to endure

fictive realities. Something propels
me on to reach the house, deep and calm
among the hills, a Sleeper, immortelle,

cupped in the Downs' accommodating palm.
A place of gatherings; not quite an end
nor yet a start. A garden like a psalm

to ease transition. Here I can depend
on anonymity, cast off the chill
of being who I am. A place to mend

all those uncertainties, re-learn the rules
of resolution, ways of being still.

7

Of resolution, ways of being still.
Having lost our grip, mislaid the crib-sheet
for our lives, we are unmanageable,

dancing in the internecine streets.
*We'll survive if we stay mobile; plot
and counter-plot will save us from defeat.*

Now we have forgotten how to stop.
This house runs tutorials in slowing
down; it organizes polyglot

diplomas, seminars in knowing
when it's time to pause, to mitigate
the temper of the present. Owing

that much to self I should co-operate,
bound to a place in which I can relate.

8

Bound to a place in which I can relate;
stringing word-palaces from room to room.
Listening. Syllables reverberate;

through the air they oscillate in perfumed
nuances. I seize them when I can,
pin them quivering to the page, assume

my role as butcher, baker, artisan
for—how long will it take?—here in this house
of curious brightness, where the pale light scans

my face as I write or sit and browse;
where morning comes white as limpid crystal
on my skin, engraved like glass as I drowse,

with feather, beak and claw. Where I reveal
anticipation of the possible.

9

Anticipation of the possible
unfurls like a sleepy cat. The air thrums,
membrane-marked by imperceptible

incisions from jagged wings that come
and go across the cerulean sky.
Birds zing like shuttles on elastic looms;

with constant busyness and poignant cry
they soak the house in contrapuntal song
and measured madrigal. They prophesy

eternal winters, crippling rain, long
periods of drought. They celebrate
rich harvests in uneven carillon.

We peck in stippled shadows, and debate
each negative examined, isolate.

10

Each negative examined, isolate.
This pack of guilt; that box of bulldozed
argument; parings of neglect; the weight

of rotting errors, sent to decompose
beyond the shrubbery, out of sight
of present circumstance. Enough to close

the gate and walk into the melting light
of scorching summer days; to watch the wren
rouse the buddleia, the teazels ringed bright

with goldfinches, the twilight bustle when
blackbird and thrush descend to entertain
their young around the pond. Enough to blend

into the shallows with unravelled pain,
to wash away misfortune's chequered stain.

11

To wash away misfortune's chequered stain
that charges lives with sharp anxiety;
to challenge thought with no thought, yet remain

receptive, open to the rarity
that one's unconscious little gods provide
through an increased suggestibility.

The garden's many voices speak aside;
an echo from the Song of Solomon.
Shuddering blue waves of the dignified

Cryptomeria; the Rose of Sharon's
starry yellow shawl; apples, spices; great
clumps of spurge; basil, thyme and tarragon;

mauve spotted orchids, wild and delicate,
encourage all that's natural, innate.

12

Encourage all that's natural, innate.
A kiln of bees with a generator
hum possess the house; I concentrate

on opening windows, slowly crossing floors.
Microscopic movements catch my eye
under the moon—froglets, ghosting raw

transparencies of veins, their struck surprise
quickening the grass. The house clears its throat.
At night I cannot sleep: you occupy

each room, your warmth and erudition quote
the principles of living under strain.
Absorbing traces of your remote

love, I wear you like an inner skin;
small breakages become composed again.

13

Small breakages become composed again:
the sorry face domestic business wears,
the sad confusion of the mind's campaign.

Our set addiction to material cares;
the power dependence builds; our silent part
as witness to the TV film that dares

record destruction while we wait. The art
of camouflage, of false despair; our trick
of stepping to one side while staring out

the century. Collective doubt, the thick
pall of shame we never quite explain.
All this, dissolving in a neutral flick

of time, allowing discontent to wane.
Small acts of wounding heal in your domain.

14

Small acts of wounding heal in your domain
as time becomes ephemeral. I cling
to what I know, and walk about the lanes

as though reprieved. Ordinary things
and deeds conceal the real significants
of life. Symbols of security in

everyday disguise, they imbibe our chance,
our suffering, with casual concern;
their textured mouths form compelling entrance

to the past; memory by touch. I turn
a page; this writing has your voice. I grow
into your coat, your chair, and keep Minden

with me, after, like a kind of charm. So:
if it's a question of leaving, just go.

15

If it's a question of leaving, just go.
To want something this much: to be this near
the confluence of water and the crow,

river of the calligraphic signature,
the earth's muscles flexing. Our free-will,
tranquillity, become a ligature

of resolution, ways of being still.
Bound to a place in which I can relate
anticipation of the possible,

each negative examined, isolate;
to wash away misfortune's chequered stain,
encourage all that's natural, innate.

Small breakages become composed again.
Small acts of wounding heal in your domain.

Apologia: Apis mellifera

White with sleep; driving inside taut, illusive skin through trails
of insensible towns, arriving with relief.
Now I put on caretaking clothes
and walk about these rooms once more,
re-learning half-forgotten resonance, the timbre
of my tread, familiar textures. Feeling the house breathe.

As the night ghosts and patters by, dark syllables rough-mouth
their way into my dreams, waking me with guttural
tut and clack. It gets me every time,
the shrunk quiet of three o'clock; the absolute black.
And then a fire-cracker, brilliant dawn: the clattering birds,
chipper horses passing up the hill; an undercurrent hum.

This house is full of bees. Surround-sound purring through the walls,
strings *vibrato*, *maestoso*. They drift in and out under the eaves,
that broken tile: obeying orders, just as I
water well, pick salad, level-up the pond,
attend to fallen leaves; tenderly remove strays from the bath
(only a few at first, as though rehearsing some Greek tragedy).

Oppressive days. The bees increase activity, emerging
on your desk, your rug, the window-sill. Twitching still.
I unlock new, hot blocks of air
but they die anyway without their queen,
a sisterhood of commas. Corpses thicken by the hour, and I'm
wincing at the soft thump of bodies dropped into a jar

for mass burial. You can care for one, not a hundred, after all.
Scooping, shovelling up the rest; and then the smoke-out
in already suffocating heat. The man
lets me photograph his murdering skill.
(I too am implicated, having made the call). Doors open
for the sweet grey fumes. The sky, now yellow as honey

and stung by lightning, gilds *Helix aspersa* as it glides
over glass in front of me, gulping watered storm;
our mouths are less than half an inch apart.
After the rain, the shock of silent flowers.
I press my ear against the bathroom wall. Nothing.
Or maybe—just a tremor, like the shiver
of a wing.

The Naming of Parts

You lent me space
when mine ran out.

A clear, silver space;
I could see my life in it.

You covered me with fine nets
to stop the dried blood

of autumn leaves
scratching my skin.

You showed me quince
one mellow afternoon;

gold scars in the soft
hills of cupped hands.

You dig together in the rain,
deftly shaping wet silence

into green pools of light.
Moving about the damp grass

you fit like the
nestling of young birds.

I want to surround myself
with your still grace,

your generous breath flickering
up the raw edge of my spine.

Back in my box,
I think of two tall women

for whom the naming of parts
suspends each little death.

OXFORD POETS

Fleur Adcock
Moniza Alvi
Joseph Brodsky
Basil Bunting
Tessa Rose Chester
Daniela Crăsnaru
Michael Donaghy
Keith Douglas
D. J. Enright
Roy Fisher
Ida Affleck Graves
Ivor Gurney
David Harsent
Gwen Harwood
Anthony Hecht
Zbigniew Herbert
Tobias Hill
Thomas Kinsella
Brad Leithauser
Derek Mahon
Jamie McKendrick

Sean O'Brien
Alice Oswald
Peter Porter
Craig Raine
Zsuzsa Rakovszky
Henry Reed
Christopher Reid
Stephen Romer
Carole Satyamurti
Peter Scupham
Jo Shapcott
Penelope Shuttle
Anne Stevenson
George Szirtes
Grete Tartler
Edward Thomas
Charles Tomlinson
Marina Tsvetaeva
Chris Wallace-Crabbe
Hugo Williams